PIECES OF ME

PIECES OF ME

A Poetry & Lyrics Collection

JESSICA EISSFELDT

Pieces of Me: A poetry & lyrics collection
Jessica Eissfeldt
Copyright © 2020 by Jessica Eissfeldt. All rights reserved.
Print Edition

ISBN: 978-1-989290-16-3

Also By Jessica Eissfeldt

Sweet Historical Romance:

Sweethearts & Jazz Nights
Dialing Dreams
Shattered Melodies
Fancy Footwork
Unspoken Lyrics
The Sweethearts & Jazz Nights Boxed Set: The Complete Collection

Love By Moonlight
Beneath A Venetian Moon
Beside A Moonlit Shore
The Love By Moonlight Boxed Set: The Complete Collection

Sweet Contemporary Romance:

Prince Edward Island Love Letters & Legends
This Time It's Forever
Now It's For Always
At Last It's True Love

Other Works

Collections

Pieces of Me: A Poetry & Lyrics Collection
Love & Lattes: A Sweet Romance Short Story Collection

Chick Lit

Love, Your Fangirl

Emotional snapshots in my own life. That's what the words on the following pages are.

Too often, I feel, novelists get hidden behind their own books; their own voices and personalities drown out in favor of those of the characters and worlds created by the novelist.

Which is why I write poetry and lyrics, and why I feel compelled to convey a sense of myself, my voice, for you, my fans, my audience, so you can understand the whys behind the stories I create.

Because I've learned that my VOICE is my brand.

Thank you for hearing my voice.

—Jessica Eissfeldt
May 1, 2020

Poetry

Historical

Louisiana Love Song

Two lovers met
One moonlight night
Back in 1862

She, a Confederate belle
And he, of Union blue

Her brother caught them
In a forbidden embrace
And called out her love to duel

Though she cried and begged him not
He knew what he must, for honor, do

But before he could tell her of his love
He lay bleeding on the sand
And even as he drew his last
He tried to press a letter into her hand...

>—Our love is true, our love is deep
>I shall be with you again
>Though I don't know when or how
>But this promise I shall keep—

PIECES OF ME

Sunlight dapples on the hood
Of that dented old Ford
She pulls onto the tree-lined drive
And holds her breath
The plantation house feels alive

She shrugs a shoulder and gets out
Iron key ring in her hand
Determination on her mind
But she shivers as she crosses
The threshold to find....

...the wind, in whispers, say:

—our love is true, our love is deep—

Up the winding, curving stairs
Covered in spider webs and dust
She climbs on until the top
She feels a breath, a phantom touch
But she turns, and there is not

She pushes open the carved ornate door
To the last room on the left
Though the hinges creak and groan
She sees a letter on the floor
And knows that she is not alone

She picks up the fragile yellowed page
Her face is all aglow

JESSICA EISSFELDT

In the light of the setting sun
She holds the words up to her heart
And, now, at last she knows:

> —Our love is true, our love is deep
> I shall be with you again
> Though I don't know when or how
> But this promise I shall keep—

Christmas Reflections

Frosted glitter brushes the eaves
As soft flakes float down

The clink of fine china
Against the sterling gleams
In the candlelight's glow

The scene
all enwreathed in fine poinsettia
And mistletoe

You smile and bring the crystal to my lips
The sweet spiced scent of the cider
Fills me as I take a heady sip

Then you slip your hand in mine
And lift it to your lips
While the fine aroma of pine
Mingles with the sharp crackle of logs in the grate

JESSICA EISSFELDT

As your gaze grazes mine
The heat spreads through my blood
You press a kiss to my palm

And I wish I could live
In this place of fantasy
Familiarity
forever

Because I still see your smile
Each time I run my hand
Along the banister
Entwined with red velvet ribbons
And shining silver stars

Because I still feel your touch
When I see the Christmas tree in
the hall
So majestic and tall
Against the holiday-hued
Oriental at my feet done in
threaded
Golds and blues

Because I can still hear your voice
when you come up behind me
and whisper "Merry Christmas" in
my ear
With your hand at my waist
The warmth of your touch on my

silk gown
Sets my heart ablaze

As the carolers sing
Of heralded glory
On high

But all I need to do is take one look
Around to see I'm in the 21st
century
Not the 19th.

So I close my eyes
Oh, why does this place
Feel so right
When it takes me back in time

—at least in my mind—

Because my heart can't ignore
This longing and yearning
For you and I and all our
Christmases before

So I sigh and step out the door

But the jingle of sleigh bells
Ringing
Sets my heart singing
when I see a shooting star

And on this frozen night
I know it's perfectly right
To honor the memories of
Christmases past

Because they will be nothing
compared
to our Christmases yet to come
when I'm in your arms again at last

Heart Wood

A willow tree
Stood
On a hill
By herself

Her roots
Deep
Her branches
Long
Her heart
Frozen
Suspended
In time

Or so she thought

Until a man
Of the forest
Came along
One day

His hair
Black

His eyes
Blue
His back
Laced
With scars
Time
Could not
Erase

Yet he sank down
On his knees
Placed a hand
On her trunk
The bark cool and still to his touch

Or so he thought

But from deep
Within
The mighty
Willow tree

She felt a
Stirring
way down
In her roots

As the man
Continued
To kneel

Before her
In sweet
Supplication

She felt
The gentle touch
Of his hand
Warming her
Through and through

And before
She could think
To try to
Understand the
Hows and the whys

Within her heart
It began:
A stirring
Became a humming
A humming
Became a whirring
Til soon she
Discovered

From the tips
Of her leaves
To the ends
Of her roots

The golden
Sap
Within her
Was flowing free
Once again

And day
After day
After day
After day
The man of the forest
Returned
To her place
On the hill
Nestled himself
Amongst her
Roots

And watered
Her with the
Tears of his
Silent pleas
Going unheard

Or so they both thought

But each day
He continued
To return
Stroking

Her bark
Sighing
Her name
His voice
Twining
Its way
Through her branches

Then on the night
Of the
Seventh moon
When he did
Return
To her spot
High on the hill
The tree
Was not there

As the moonlight
Shone down
Making a path
For
His steps
Heavy
His heart
Lead

But as he turned
To go

JESSICA EISSFELDT

Blossoms
Burst forth
On the hill
As far as
His eye could see

And up from
The ground
On her spot
On the hill
Came a woman
All clothed
In gold
Her hair
brown
Her eyes
green
And he knew
It was his
Touch, and his words, and his tears
That had
healed her heart
and broken
the spell

forever
at last

They ran

Down
The hill
together

JESSICA EISSFELDT

To Her Beloved:

Love, oh love, oh love
The dawn of the first sunrise
Never looked so sweet as thou dost

A million diamond sunsets
Rest between now and then
Then and now
Past and future

But what is the future
But tomorrow's present
A gift to be opened, explored,
discovered

Within the moments, seconds, eons
of tomorrow's yesterday
That heady yesterday's yearning
Turned sunlight

Oh love, oh love oh love
Why dost thou elude me?

PIECES OF ME

Nay, nay, nay
Show not thy simple ways
Yet thy harp's heartstrings spun
fine as golden sunshine
True-pointed clear crystal
Cold as the first star of even'tide

Make love to me
thy cool sweet lips
Thy dewy velvet touch
Thy caresses rich as nectar
Deep as shadow
Hidden as twilight

Oh love, oh love, oh love
How doth I long for thy touch
Thy word
Thy promised vow

And tomorrow, tomorrow,
tomorrow
Ah sweet yesterday's future
promise

Risen from the grave of lost hopes
Timid dreams and
Fragile joys

Nay, nay, nay
Calleth me not a fool

For it lies not in thine own breast
but in mine own
This sweet honeyed longing
Full of tomorrow's promises

Wrapped like jewels in the finest
linen
Only brought forth for the fairest of
merry occasions
Guarded by many-hinged locks and
intricate seamless satin pouches,
Veiled raiments and rainbow-hued
love-notes

Sweet drops on the soul of this
parched earth
Tis not nightfall yet
Though I doth I feel as if it might be
A hundred thousands eons of time
passed on parchment before I set
eyes on thou

The faint scratch of a feather quill
Pronounces our future together
As husband and wife
And yet I wait
Perched on my velvet cushion

Breathing in the dew of morning,
The sweet fog of night

PIECES OF ME

The hungry vapors of nightfall's
rapt attention to those sparkling
spectres, the stars

Far above and yet too far below
Touched and yet not touched

Seen and yet not seen
Hidden and yet clear as day

Clear as a bell
Clear as crystal
Yet fogged like the harbor when
ships pull anchor

Oh love, oh love oh love
How I dost crave thy touch

Thy tender ministrations
Thy honeyed tones
Thy velvet voice

Bound up in so many gold-leafed
pages
Of magic, fantasy, dragons and
princes
Yet what dost my heart tell me?

JESSICA EISSFELDT

To his beloved:

Pray tell, sweet heart, sweet center
of my soul
Pray tell for I shall listen, as I
always have, as I always will.
Long not for me for thou do
knowest that thee and I are forever
together

Sweet beauty, trouble not thy brow
with sorrow
Raise not that silken kerchief to thy
rose-hued cheek
Raise not thy voice in anguish

Wipe away those diamond
dewdrops springing so easily from
thine eyes
For I am always thine
I am always here
Trust me, trust thyself
Trust thine own true heart to tell
thou, to show thou that eternal
truth

PIECES OF ME

Thoust cravings are not in vain
I hear all, see all, touch all, feel all.
Thou art me and I art thou.

Sweet lovely, fear not, fear not
Thou art precious, cherished,
honored and surrounded
By legions of angels
Pouring their love out in
Liquid gold for you

So lift up thy lips into a smile, into
joyful thoughts and sweet refrains
Fear not for I am with thee
always and forever.

Family

House on the Hill

House on the hill
You're with me still

Even though now
I'll never again
Know the bright bobbing
Of your geranium pots in pinks and reds
All lined up on that old stone wall

House on the hill
You're with me still
Even though now
I'll never again smell the sweet aroma
Of freshly mowed grass
Or roll down the hill tumbling
Through laughter and sunshine
Or stand on that billion-year-old
Big old rock in the corner of the lawn

House on the hill
You're with me still
Even though now

PIECES OF ME

I'll never look up at the basketball net
Nailed to that old oak tree
Beside the secret stone steps
That lead to the cool basement
Where I played tiddly-winks and drew cats on the chalkboard

House on the hill
You're with me still
Even though now
I'll never again feel the warm welcoming pavement
Beneath my flowered Keds
When I'd jump out of the car
one summer holiday after another
Year after year

> The drive never grew old
> Even though I grew older each year
> There was still something thrilling about
> That curvy hilly drive
> Where I would arrive at the big house on the hill
>
> Where candy and popsicles and ice cream awaited
> And the spicy scent of spaghetti sauce

Bubbled over the stove
Stirred with love and sprinkled
    with kisses

House on the hill
You're with me still
Even though now
I'll never again see the wild turkeys
    through the trees
Or the petunias blooming by the
    hedge
Or hear the crows caw through the
    second-story window

Because some stranger bought you
And moved in

Not aware that the little girl inside
    me
Still longs to curl up with that black
    and gray
knitted afghan on the crinkly
    leather couch
the sweet smell of warm laundry
    tickling her nose
as she rose to give her grandma a
    kiss on the cheek

Now, will some other little girl

PIECES OF ME

Slide down that red carpet on the stairs
early on Saturday morning
To watch cartoons?

Or watch in awe and wonder the Christmas lights
glisten from the branches
Of that big old pine draped with glittering snow?

Now of course I'll never know

But I'd like to think
That maybe she'll also get to peek
behind the door on Easter
And find that basket of candy

Or maybe her own grandmother
Will take her out shopping
Smiling and singing all the way
Down the hill

Oh, house on the hill
You're with me still
If only in my heart

Singing In The Car On The Way Down The Hill

You singing in the car
On the way down the hill
Even after all these years
I remember it, still

Now that you're gone

You laughing in the kitchen
Pasta boiling on the stove
Even after all these years
I remember it, still

Now that you're gone.

The scent of spices
And pine trees
And hand cream…

Now that you're gone

Us making lambie cake
And me eating every jelly bean

PIECES OF ME

Christmas and Thanksgiving
And Easter; candlelight and
silverware and family;
treats and delights all around
in the house on the hill
Even after all these years
I remember it, still.

Now that you're gone.

Oh how clearly I remember
Now that you're gone

Laughter and pasta
And that smile of yours
Teaching me the finer points; that
beauty's all around

And how precious
These memories shine
To tuck away
In my mind
Taken out to cherish
Taken out to treasure
Now that you're gone

And all the love
And the laughter
That you left behind
Still somehow echo

JESSICA EISSFELDT

Down the hallways
The pathways of my mind

Because...
I'll be singing in the car
on the way down the hill
even after all these years
I'll remember it, still.

Love & kisses, Grandma
Thank you for everything you did for
me, for all the love
And the lessons.
May you be at peace
In the land of golden light

JVSE: 1915-2015

The Writing Process

The Word Catcher

Why, the imagination of a writer
Is a rare creature indeed

Just tell her what you want
And she will get you what you need

Searching, and lurking and
searching some more
Until all the ideas she's collected
Won't even fit through your door!

So you put on your writing cap
Strap it on real tight

And jump into that jungle
to slay the words
that don't fill you with delight

You toss and you turn
And you whirl around
Every one of those letters
That your imagination has found

PIECES OF ME

Til none but the
Very best
Come out with the perfect right
sound

And then you'll discover
This whole world that you've
created
Is something indeed
To be celebrated

Peopled and populated
With ideas galore!

Overflowing with thoughts
You never thought you had, before!

Whistled, whispered, doodled
And daydreamed
All over the floor

Yes, they're weirdly wonderfully
Wackily
Writerly words!

Flocks and flocks and
Stacks and stacks of them
Grouped together in herds

They're in all colors
And shapes and in all sizes too

JESSICA EISSFELDT

Long strings of words
Some even painted to look just like you

Yes, they're floating up there on the breeze
And you can pick them out
As easy as you please

But only if you're sure to take
the very best
Flight

Because if you're not careful
These words, well, these words
Could just disappear out of sight!

So you need to very gently
Approach them—preferably at night
When they're all
Snug in their little sentence-diagram beds
With visions of dictionaries
Dancing through their heads

So you reach out and extend your word-catcher net
And look, oh, just look
You've caught
The very best, tip-top, bestest word yet!

<u>Content Edit</u>

Hey editor,
I'm not content
With your content edit

How could you say
My writing was crap?

Now I want
To scrap
Everything
I've ever written

And lock up my heart
In a box
Marked
Writer's block

And never come out
Ever.

You told me I used
Too many exclamation
Points!

Called my work
"Juvenile"
and
"autobiographical"

(Okay, so maybe I'm proving your point
right now with this poem)

But at least
Now I know who to blame
When I eat
That whole chocolate cake
I baked

In one sitting

Hey editor
I heard
getting the last word
is the best revenge

So.
There.

New York

Downtown Dinner Date

I want to slide to the floor
With him
Like the melting butter in the pan

Instead
I run a hand
Along the maple surface
Of his smooth satiny
Cutting board
The wood silky
Under my fingertips

He smiles
As he slices
As if he knows…

That blue-eyed gaze
Flashing
So many
Fantasies
Gone unfulfilled
Until tonight

PIECES OF ME

In his Manhattan mansion

He hands me the knife
The snowy linen
Of his shirtsleeves
rolled to reveal that smooth skin

I take a step
closer,
See the way he leans against the
counter
His fingers
Close on mine.

"Like this,"
his breath caresses
my cheek,
his hand guides mine
on the handle
of the knife
as he steps in behind

Oh
God.

"Like this?"
I turn my eyes to his
the blade
heavy in my hands
the flash of steel

in the candlelight

His spicy cologne
And the zip of onion
fill my head

"Yes,"
his lips nip
my neck,
my ear.

Oh
God.

Butter sizzles in the pan
His hands,
his eyes,
his lips

Pressed up against the counter
Can't think
Can't breath
Can only feel
The warmth of his
Arms around my waist

"Oh yes,"
His words
my lips
"just"

sliding
"like"
clinging
"this"
moist and hot

The onions fall
Translucent
Tiny pieces
Scattered
to the floor.

Manhattan Morning

His black hair flows
Like watered silk.
Shining, alive.

Falling down over his brow
A single strand,
Freed from that perfectly mussed
coif.

As he stands at the sink
Splashing sleep from his face
The wet drops cling to the living
marble of his skin
While the morning sun streams
through the leaded glass window,
Illuminating every seamless curve.
Every perfect angle.

Divine. Heavenly, even.
Yet so masculine.
A heady combination, I decide
As a sigh whispers past my lips.

PIECES OF ME

I feel like I should
be quoting Shakespeare. Voltaire.

But all I can do is stare
At the aquamarine jewels that are
his eyes.
Such a deep, clear, crystal blue
Just waiting to be dived into.
Those waters the only assuage to
my heady fever.

I take a step nearer.
Watch as he brings a towel to his
face,
Wiping away that last vestige of
moisture.

But one daring droplet escapes,
Gleefully sliding down his
sandpaper jawline,
Its path unhindered
On a route my fingers yearn to
follow.

The wet bead skims
Over the strong muscles of his neck
That will soon smell like Armani
aftershave
And be kissed by the pressed collar
of his $5,000 shirt.

JESSICA EISSFELDT

It glides over his collarbone,
The long lithe structure
That hints at challenges
Carried gracefully. Smoothly.
Like a river ribboning its way
through a deep canyon.

The drop comes next
To the broad flat expanse of his chest
That the New York dawn gilds
A rich honeyed hue.

Unerringly, the drop keeps its course
Along his abdomen
Then seems to pause.
– Oh –
What a place to dally.

A space surely the work of Old Masters
Who sat patiently with their chisels
Until the purity of the white stone came alive,
Illuminated by the spirit within,
A soft glow glimmering
Beneath the surface.

Their masterpiece

of blood, bone, skin and sinew.

But the droplet moves on
Until it reaches the terrycloth barrier
of the 1,000-thread-count cotton towel
Tucked firmly around his waist.

Though I hold my breath
The bold droplet does not hesitate
But plunges under those soft folds
To a place of ultimate power.
Supreme virility.
A place full of potent magic
Just waiting to be released.

My skin grows hot
At the thought.

Then I spot the tiny speck of moisture
Appear just below his knee,
Arriving at the bunched muscles of his calf.

No one since Hermes,
Or even Zeus himself,
Could ever hope to dream
Of having such poised strength

Propelling him forward with every step.

The droplet then curves around his ankle
That juts jauntily
Just like his trademark fedora.

Until finally, finally
The drop lands with a satisfied splat
On the bare floorboards.

He looks up.
Turns to me.
And smiles.

Love Life

Shane

On that college campus
In that ivy-covered brick building
Full of knowledge and learning
My nose was in a book
But my head was wrapped
In thoughts of you

Your brown hair half-hiding your eyes
So intelligent
And the solid lines of your broad back
Sitting there in that corner seat
So masculine

You spoke commandingly about
Keats
And Yeats
But all I could think of
Were your romantic feats

PIECES OF ME

Would you kiss me at the chalkboard,
Up against the words of Shelley and Shakespeare?

Or would we do group work
For two
Late into the night?
Oh yes, my Critical Analysis
Class project—was you.

All semester long.

And when finals came
I wished I could finely examine
My curiosity
About the feel of your stubble
Under my fingertips

Alas, that bell never rang.

But at least I've
Finally examined
My desire
For you
Ten years
Too late

Cashmere Sweater

Saturday morning
You come in
Looking like sunshine
And smelling like—well, I don't
know—since I'm behind the
counter

And you're miles away, or so it
seems
Because you've come
To use the computer

Instead of checking *me* out
Even though I work at the library

Sigh.
You're so good looking
But it's not looking good for me
Because you just politely
Say hello
In that sexy foreign accent
And then log in to your account

PIECES OF ME

Guess there's no accounting
For taste
Though yours is obviously
impeccable
In that blue cashmere sweater that I
imagine matches your eyes

Why do you come here every day?
Are you an exiled prince of some
European nation-state I've never
heard of?
Or are you some dot-com
billionaire who went bust?

I don't quite know why I'm making
such a fuss
because I know you're probably
neither of those; it's just…

I sneak a covert glance
Then make it seem like chance
When I just happen
To shelve some large print books
On your side of the room

As I line the books up on the shelf
I secretly congratulate myself
For wearing my hair down today
I love the way it feels:
loose and free and thick

And I can't help but wonder
If your eyes wander to it, too
To watch it sway and shine and mesmerize
And can't you help but wonder
Whether it feels like silk
Beneath your fingertips?

I slip back into my seat
take a sip of tea
Bring myself back to reality
Then realize with a jolt
Our eyes just met

Perhaps there's hope yet...

A Sexy Crooner

There once was a sexy crooner named Matt.
Who was more mischievous than a cat.
Every showtime at dusk, he sang & he swayed
For every crowd that he ever played.
Now how could he be more awesome than that?

Tears Glisten

Tears glisten
Where there used to be smiles
Guess I should be happy
To have all the memories

But all I can see is the sadness
Of what might have been
Now turned to dust

Ashes from hope
And bitterness from laughter
Torn apart by
too little money
And too much time

Gone, gone
All is gone

Scattered to the four directions
And lost on the wind

And it feels like a sin

PIECES OF ME

When I think of all those happy times

Now nothing more
Than fragile memories
pressed between the layers of my broken heart

And now it's too late
I can't go back
But can't go forward yet

Must quietly wait and wait and wait some more

Until perhaps, like cocoons into butterflies,
the fabric of my heart is healed

Hope and new possibilities will be set free in time and in sunshin

I Won't Abandon You

(For M.K.)

Your couch
Our conversation

Black curls
Brown eyes
One look
Oh, so much

Talk turns to touch

One word
Two hearts

Sweaty skin
Twisted sheets
Whispered touch

Best night
City lights
I kiss your throat
And you say

"I won't abandon you"

Dawn's rays
Warm gaze

"I won't abandon you"

JESSICA EISSFELDT

That Australian Smile

Dan,
You were the man
Who I never thought
I'd fall for

With your shaved head
And your steel-rimmed glasses
Like some sort of Superman
In a soft gray t-shirt
And sexy Australian accent

You defied
My conventions

But when you stood
Too close to me
In that art
Gallery

I knew I was nowhere near
Far enough
From you
To prevent

PIECES OF ME

My falling
For you

And when you smiled
That smile
That way
That was
My cue

To run far and fast
Because somehow
I couldn't comprehend
Being with someone
Who was
So nice
And called himself
Atheist

Yet you were different
You wanted to hold all my secrets
And for that I was afraid

So that's why I said goodbye
After three dates
And one email
explaining how my spirituality
Wasn't in alignment
With your reality

And you thanked me

JESSICA EISSFELDT

For being the first woman to
explain to you why
she'd decided to end it with you
But I can't begin
To explain
To myself

Why, now
After five years
Of taking myself
Out for coffee
A differing
Worldview
was so Very Important
After all

After all,
Don't we
All just want a
Happy ending?

Wish I could rewind time
Then maybe
Your Australian smile
Would be with me still

Dream of You

Last night I dreamt of you
We lay with twisted sheets
And tangled hearts

Why does it seem
So real to me
When I dream of you

And when will it be
That I can see you
In the flesh at last?

When I dream of you
When I dream of you

But when I wake
I feel so sad
You aren't there

But I dream of you
But I dream of you

Is this all I'll ever get?

These pieces and snatches in my sleep
Of a love so true
It feels so deep

When I dream of you
When I dream of you

When I dream of you
When I dream of you

Give my love
to you, beloved

when I dream of you
when I dream of you

Untitled

I feel your touch
On my skin
And this feeling
Begins

Coursing
Through
My veins

And I know now
Nothing will
Ever be the same
It's the way
You say my name
It's the way
You see me
In the dark
And I can feel
My heart
Begin
To open and expand
With every

JESSICA EISSFELDT

Touch of your hand

You're opening me
Up inside
So that I have
No where to hide
No place to stand
Except in the glow
Of your love
Pouring down
On me from above

I put up walls
To try to stall
My own heart
Got the boundaries
Confused
With the safety
Of the walls
I'd built around
My heart

But now
I feel your touch
On my skin
And this feeling
Begins

Lyrics

Til You Came Along

My life wasn't a song
Thought I didn't belong
My baby'd just left
And I was bereft
Til you came along

Back then I didn't know
If I'd finish the show
Or just have to go
I as filled with woe
Til you came along

Now it's a brand new refrain
Cuz it's sure we're one and the same
I didn't know what I was missin'
And I confess I'm reminisc'n
There was nothing so dear
But babe now that you're here
I see it so clear

Cuz you came along

A Second Look (I'm the kind of girl with her nose in a book)

You came in
To the library
Returned your books
Then looked at me

I didn't know
What to say
So I looked back down
At this page

Cuz I'm the kind of girl
With her nose in a book
Too scared to
Take a second look
At you looking at me

You've passed my seat
So many times
While I've been writing here

Cuz I'm the kind of girl

With her nose in a book
Too scared to
Take a second look
At you looking at me

So today I ripped
This poem
From my notebook
And handed it to you
As you walked by
And now you know why

I'm the kind of girl
With her nose in a book
Consider this my second look
At you looking at me

PIECES OF ME

An Experiment Gone Wrong

No I don't want a lecture
And I'm not a student of yours
If you'd listen for half a second
There's more to hear
Than the sound of your own fears

Oh you've caused me
Such confusion
You're as indecipherable
As nuclear fusion
Am I so bad at chemistry
I'd mistaken this for that?
Thank God I'm through with science class
Cuz this is
An experiment gone wrong

The thing I don't understand
Is why you called me illogical and
    incomprehensible
Yet I felt confused and abused
By your circular questions
And your misperceptions

And this was all before
We'd even met in real life...

Oh you've caused me
Such confusion
You're as indecipherable
As nuclear fusion
Am I so bad at chemistry
I'd mistaken this for that?
Thank God I'm through with science class
Cuz this is
An experiment gone wrong

I don't need this kind of drama
Is it only a product of my past trauma
Or yours?

Placing blame is a two-timing game
I don't want to have to play with you
But you forced my hand
Oh you've caused me
Such confusion
You're as indecipherable
As nuclear fusion
Am I so bad at chemistry
I'd mistaken this for that?
Thank God I'm through with science class
Cuz this is
An experiment gone wrong

There's no textbook
For this kind of thing
Guess I'll have to invent
A way to heal my heartstrings, cuz...

You've caused me
Such confusion
You're as indecipherable
As nuclear fusion
Am I so bad at chemistry
I'd mistaken this for that?
Thank God I'm through with science class
Cuz this is
An experiment gone wrong

Tall, Dark-Haired and Handsome

Tied on my skates
On that very first date with you
My heart got all fluttery
Cuz, man, I could feel the chemistry
Between you and me

Oh, tall, dark-haired and handsome
You were just what
I'd been waiting for
Oh how I wanted the chance
To explore these feelings for you more

I thought, wow
This could really be great
Until I had to go
And stupidly hesitate
When you asked me
If we could extend our date
By maybe getting a bite to eat
But by then it was too late...

Oh, tall, dark-haired and handsome

PIECES OF ME

You were just what
I'd been waiting for
Oh how I wanted the chance
To explore these feelings for you more

Did you think I wasn't interested
Is that why you gave me your number
Instead of asking me for mine?

But maybe there's a
Happy ending
To this story after all
Cuz I've just picked up
My phone right now
And I'm giving you a call

Oh, tall, dark-haired and handsome
You're just what
I've been waiting for
Maybe now I'll get the chance
To explore these feelings for you more

JESSICA EISSFELDT

If I'd Said Yes

I stood by my suitcase
Waiting for the bus
Watched you from a distance
And then you came up

We got to talking
That bus it didn't show
So tell me, I have to know...

If I'd said yes
To your offer of a ride
Would my hair be blowing
In the California wind
With you forever by my side?

Our easy conversation
And your warm brown eyes
Made me want to unpack my luggage
And spend my life under sunny skies

If I'd said yes
To your offer of a ride
Would my hair be blowing

PIECES OF ME

In the California wind
With you forever by my side?

Can close my eyes
Still feel that San Diego sun
Why did I hold myself back
From having maybe
More than fun?

If I hadn't
Then maybe now
I'd be sitting by your side...

Oh, If I'd said yes
To your offer of a ride
Would my hair be blowing
In the California wind
With you forever by my side?

Ex

I open up my email
And see your name
But I can already feel
The flames in my heart

Cuz I told you we were over
I told you we were through
So what the hell are you
Trying to do?

You're my ex, ex, ex
So I'm putting x's through your name
Why do you feel the need
To come back and try to stake a claim?
Well the only stake you'll get
Is on through your heart
If you try to start something
With me again

I open up my door
And see you're there
But I know that look

PIECES OF ME

And every trick in your little black book

You're my ex, ex, ex
So I'm putting x's through your name
Why do you feel the need
To come back and try to stake a claim?
Well the only stake you'll get
Is on through your heart
If you try to start something
With me again

Five years ago
You pretended to care
While you sucked out my secrets
And drained my dreams dry
But now

You're my ex, ex, ex
So I'm putting x's through your name
Why do you feel the need
To come back and try to stake a claim?
Well the only stake you'll get
Is on through your heart
If you try to start something
With me again

Well the only stake you'll get
Is one through your heart – so don't even start

Shades of Gray

As you lean against the lamppost
And offer me a light
I shake my head
Cuz good girls don't
But I've got you
I can see it in your blue eyes

Think I'm so sure
Think I'm so right
Think everything about you
Is all black and white

Like a fog creeping through the night
You push me past
My comfort zone
Into these shades of gray
Yet something about this
Feels so right

So you asked me to the movies
And even held the door
Cuz that's what good guys do

But there's more to see here
Than just a picture show

But is there
Nothing to our connection
Than smoke and mirrors and the sound of
 my own fears?

Like a fog creeping through the night
You push me past
My comfort zone
Into these shades of gray
Yet something about this
Feels so right

One by one
Your dark secrets come out as
As we're lying side by side
But you bring me flowers
And we talk for yours
With your heart on your sleeve

Oh black and white has me blue
Cuz I don't know
What to do about you

Like a fog creeping through the night
You push me past
My comfort zone
Into these shades of gray

Yet something about this
Feels so right

Now somewhere in these shades of gray
I find myself
In love with you
Cuz you're not the enemy
I was so sure you were…
No, the world's not all black and white
And this isn't a film noir

No, the world's not all black and white
And this isn't a film noir

Last Night (You Swept Me Off My Feet)

When you took me
For that ride
I wondered if I could
Let my heart decide
Oh, how I wanted
To open up inside

Well, last night
You swept me
Off my feet
While I was
Sitting on your couch
Cuz looking into
Your blue eyes
I felt myself
Let go of doubt

I shared my secrets
In your living room
As the music played
And you let me stay

Wrapped up in your arms
That's why...
Well, last night

You swept me
Off my feet
While I was
Sitting on your couch
Cuz looking into
Your blue eyes
I felt myself
Let go of doubt

So this is me
Telling you
I think I want to
Walk through
That open door
With you. Cuz...

Well, last night
You swept me
Off my feet
While I was
Sitting on your couch
Cuz looking into
Your blue eyes
I felt myself
Let go of doubt

www.ingramcontent.com/pod-product-compliance
Lightning Source LLC
Chambersburg PA
CBHW020543080526
44583CB00013B/977